Little Too-Tall

by Jane Belk Moncure
illustrated by Linda Hohag
and Dan Spoden

Published by
THE CHILD'S WORLD®

Mankato, Minnesota

GROLIER
B O O K S

Grolier Books is a division of
Grolier Enterprises, Inc.,
Danbury, CT.

The Library —
A Magic Castle

Come to the magic castle
When you are growing tall.
Rows upon rows of Word Windows
Line every single wall.
They reach up high,
As high as the sky,
And you want to open them all.
For every time you open one,
A new adventure has begun.

Scott opened a Word Window.
Guess what he saw?

Little Too-Tall . . .

all alone
in the jungle.
"I wish I had a
friend," she said.

Just then . . .

a parrot flew by.

"Hi," called out Little Too-Tall.
"Will you be my friend?"

"My word," said Parrot. . . .

"You are a funny-looking bird. Your legs are too tall. You cannot fly at all. Toodle-loo."

And away he flew.

9

Then Little Too-Tall
saw a monkey
up in a tree.

"Hi," said Little Too-Tall.
"Will you be my friend?"

"My word," said Monkey. "You are a funny-looking bird. Your neck is too long. You cannot climb a tree. Chee, chee."

Away went Monkey.

A hippo came by on his way for a swim.

"Hi," said Little Too-Tall. "Will you be my friend?"

Hippo said, "My word. You are a funny-looking bird. Your eyes are too big. You cannot swim at all."

Away went Hippo with a splash.

"I cannot swim like Hippo—or climb like Monkey—or fly like Parrot. But . . .

I can run," said Little Too-Tall.

And she did. She ran right out of the jungle . . .

and into a grassy field.

Far away, Zebra and Antelope
were eating grass.

Little Too-Tall
stood very still . . .

with her long neck high above the
grass. Suddenly, she saw . . .

a hungry lion, hiding in the grass.

Little Too-Tall ran past the lion
as fast as her tall legs would go.

"Run, Zebra. Run, Antelope. Run away
from Lion," said Little Too-Tall.

And all three dashed away to safety.

"You saved us from Lion," said Zebra.
"Please stay with us."

"Don't you think I am a funny-looking bird?" asked Little Too-Tall.

23

"My eyes
are too big.
My neck
is too long.
My legs
are too
tall."

"Not at all," said Antelope.

"With your big eyes

and your
long neck

and your
tall legs,

you are just the right size.

You can see Lion when he hides
in the grass."

"We like you just the way you are," said Zebra.

"You do?" asked Little Too-Tall.
"Then I will stay."

"And we can all be friends," said
Antelope and Zebra.

Little Too-Tall laughed one happy
laugh and hopped two happy hops.

You can read the special message on
Little Too-Tall's tail feathers with . . .

Antelope

and Zebra.